IMAGES OF ENGLAND

CHIPPING NORTON
VOLUME II

IMAGES OF ENGLAND

CHIPPING NORTON
VOLUME II

BRENDA MORRIS & ALAN WATKINS

TEMPUS

Frontispiece: The chain of the Mayor of Chipping Norton which was given to the borough by Albert Brassey MP of Heythrop House in 1897 in commemoration of the Diamond Jubilee of Queen Victoria. Names and dates of each Mayor are engraved on the links of the chain, starting with Alderman A. A. Webb, followed by Albert Brassey, Mayor in 1898.

First published 2003

Tempus Publishing Limited
The Mill, Brimscombe Port,
Stroud, Gloucestershire, GL5 2QG
www.tempus-publishing.com

© Chipping Norton Museum, 2003

The right of Brenda Morris and Alan Watkins to be identified
as the Authors of this work has been asserted in accordance
with the Copyrights, Designs and Patents Act 1988.

British Library Cataloguing in Publication Data.
A catalogue record for this book is available from the British Library.

ISBN 0 7524 2479 3

Typesetting and origination by Tempus Publishing Limited.
Printed in Great Britain by Midway Colour Print, Wiltshire.

Contents

Children are sledging down New Street in the Great Snow of 1947. The George Inn and the Blue Lion Inn are on the left-hand side of the street. The third public house, the King William, is now a fish and chip shop.

Introduction

Chipping Norton town is set 650ft above sea-level on the northern part of the Cotswold range. It is in many respects a typical Cotswold town, both in appearance and history. It is a town of great antiquity. The presence of the nearby Rollright Stones suggests that the site is one which would commend itself to that ancient race which chose the tops of hills for their dwelling places. Roman coins have been found in the vicinity and a head carved in stone has been found in the locality of Glyme Farm. This head can now be viewed in our excellent town museum.

'Chipping Norton' is a corruption of the Saxon words 'Ceapen' – to buy or cheapen – and 'Neprune' – Northmen: so it really means the 'market of the Northmen'.

There is little to be heard of events in Chipping Norton after the Domesday survey – though a castle was erected here, probably in the reign of King Stephen – the remains of which can still be seen on the 'Castle Banks'. These grassy mounds are located near to St Mary's church. A medieval arrowhead was found some years ago near this site.

King John granted a charter to the lord of the manor, giving him liberty to hold a fair at Chipping Norton for four days every year, and the town formerly had the right to send two members to Parliament, until the people petitioned to be released from this privilege owing to the expense involved.

The borough was incorporated on 27 February 1606 and was governed by two bailiffs and twelve burgesses. There was also a right given by the charter to have two sergeants-at-mace.

In the old coaching days Chipping Norton was a resting place for the coaches running between Worcester and London and was well-provided with inns for the accommodation of both man and beast. It has been said that Samuel Johnson and Boswell both frequented the posting-house at Chapel House, half a mile east of the town. It was at Chapel House that Dr Johnson in 1776 delivered his famous panegyric on taverns. 'There is no private house' he said, 'in which people can enjoy themselves so well as a capital tavern … you are sure you are welcome, and the more noise you make, the more trouble you give, the more good things you call for, the welcomer you are.' Queen Victoria and her mother, the Duchess of Kent, slept at Chapel House around the year 1886 when passing through the neighbourhood.

The Common was first granted to the inhabitants by Lord Arundell (whose family owned the Manor of Chipping Norton from the Conquest to the time of Edward III), in the year that Richard the Lionheart became King.

The parish church of St Mary's is built in the Perpendicular style and is of great interest and beauty. It is a reminder of the days when Chipping Norton was the centre of a flourishing woollen industry. The hexagonal porch is one of only three in the country.

The Guildhall, standing down just below the main road, is one of the most picturesque old buildings in the town with its characteristic Tudor windows. It has served various purposes – formerly having been described as 'The Guildhouse in Le Middell Street'. It is now used as offices by the Chipping Norton Town Council and the West Oxfordshire District Council.

Chipping Norton has been extremely fortunate in having had several early photographers in the nineteenth century to whom we are indebted as they have captured the growth of the town from a sleepy borough into a large working town. In the early twentieth century the work of Percy Simms and Frank Packer led to a profusion of landscapes, portraits and wedding pictures showing the population, streets and events of the town. It is largely owing to their endeavours, with the many thousands of photographs they took, that we have been able to select material for this book. In this volume of photographs we have concentrated on the second half of the twentieth century – mostly taken from the archives of the Chipping Norton Museum of Local History. We hope you enjoy it!

Brenda Morris

Acknowledgements

These photographs are from the collection of the Chipping Norton Museum of Local History, and from the private collections of members of the Local History Society. We would also like to thank the many people who have lent us photographs for inclusion in this volume.

Thanks are also due to the late Mrs Gwendoline Walden, for giving us the copyright for photographs in the museum taken by her father, the late Mr Frank Packer.

one

The 1940s

The coaches are stuck in the deep snow on the Oxford Road, 1947.

Prisoners of war helping to clear the snow from the A34 near Chalford Oaks in 1947.

Snow clearance at Over Norton, 1947.

The snow of 1947 melted, causing the Common brook to flood.

Above: Market Street, Chipping Norton, 1947. These pictures were drawn by Mr Conrad Gries. Conrad Gries was a German prisoner of war who was housed at Greystones, Chipping Norton in 1946/47. Conrad was stationed as a young soldier on the occupied Channel Island of Alderney. His main task was as a military draughtsman and surveyor. He was also a talented artist. After the liberation of the Channel Islands Conrad was sent to a prisoner of war camp at Chipping Norton.

Conrad made several sketches of the town and the surrounding area. He says of that time 'In 1946/47 we really loved your little fine old town and the people too, they were always very fair to us POWs. The treatment at all times was very good and I don't forget the Christmas Eve in 1946/47 when we walked along the market place. Spontaneously, a lot of your people gave us chocolates, cigarettes and little gifts so we had a real Christmas and a good hope too.'

In 1988 Conrad and another POW, Erwin, visited Chipping Norton and the camp at Greystones, but there were no more Nissen huts. When he was repatriated, he spent several years working on the restoration of churches in Germany.

Opposite above: Prisoner of war huts at Greystones, 1947.

Opposite below: Chipping Norton Town Hall, 1947.

P Jones P.O.W Camp 43 (F)
Greystone, Chipping Norton
England . 17.5.42

Chipping No
Town-He
England

Children at the British School, New Street, 1948. From left to right, back row: Derek Cox, Terence Stowe, Lionel Howes, Geoffrey Robinson, Robert Knight, John Burford, Terry Caswell, Dennis Aries, Brian Withers. Front row: Jennifer Smith, Margaret Cox, Ann Coleman, Vivienne Campbell, Veronica Jones, Irene Oliver.

Children at the British School, New Street. From left to right, back row: Beverley Epton, Kathleen Preece, Carol Strong, Suzanne Vinall, Sarah Jane Ashmore, Patricia Hayward. Middle row: Darrell Lord, Frances Jarvis, Mary Thomson, Brian Hicks, Paul Collier, Ian Day, Ann Morris, Ann Peachey, Michael Waters. Front row: Marion Reeves, Jean Turner, Susan Kitchen, Marion Rimell, Daphne Williams, Sheila Worvill, Christine Smith.

National Children's Home Fête 1948 opened by the Mayoress of Banbury. Included in the photograph are the Mayor and Mayoress of Chipping Norton, Mr and Mrs Harold Lord, Sister Little of the NCH&O and the Rev. Rollinson from the Baptist Chapel.

Staff from the Pearl Assurance Company enjoying their staff dinner in 1949.

The Women's Land Army hostel, Burford Road, Chipping Norton, formerly the hospital of RAF Chipping Norton.

The British School, New Street. From left to right, back row: George Hicks, Jean Andrews, Rose Greathead, Sheila Smith, Valerie Thomson, Brenda Campbell, Catherine Clacy, Jean Hawtin, David Tarrant. Middle row: John Edginton, Peter Hiett, Michael Benfield, Ian Hawtin, Sidney Timms, Rodney Collier, Robert Townley, Robert Nurden, David Barnes, Peter Mackenzie, John Sanders. Front row: Anita Harrison, Vivienne Gibbs, Peggy Guy, Rita Swann, Janice Dix, Brenda Mitchell, Valerie Pickett, Pat Withers, Diana Stowe.

The staff of Chipping Norton Grammar School. From left to right, back row: Joyce Stockford (Secretary), -?-, Miss Davies, -?-, Mr Lush, Mr Venn, -?-, Mr Eccleshall. Front row: Miss Venn, Miss Harrop, Miss Ellis, Miss Jones, Mr Coomber, Mr Miles, Mr Watts and Mr Partridge.

In 1947 Chipping Norton held a road safety campaign in the centre of the town.

The audience lined the streets from the Burford Corner to the top of New Street.

Several accidents were enacted and demonstrations were given on road safety.

To conclude, all the schoolchildren were given a copy of the Highway Code.

The Remembrance Day Parade 1948, with the Mayor standing on the town hall steps. Chipping Norton Silver Band are in attendance.

Mayor Harold Lord takes the salute of the Armistice Parade with Dr Russell as Parade Commander. Members of the borough council are in attendance.

two

The 1950s

Left, below and opposite above: The town hall was gutted by a fire on 3 March 1950.

Light refreshments were provided by the Co-operative café to the firemen.

The installation in the Co-operative Hall of the first lady mayor of the Borough of Chipping Norton, Miss S. A. Webb. Among those pictured are Mayoress Mrs Constance King, Mr Harold Lord, Jack Marshall, George Hannis and other members of the borough council.

The reopening ceremony of the town hall, after it had been gutted by fire, by Miss Sybil Webb, Lady Mayor and other local dignitaries.

Chipping Norton & District Allotment and Garden Association Flower Show and Fête, 1950. The presentation of cups to the winners, including Mr Doods-Parker MP, Miss Sybil Webb and Mrs Constance King.

The Punch and Judy show given by Mr Fred Lewis at the Chipping Norton & District Allotment Fête in 1950.

Members of the borough council returning from church on Remembrance Sunday 1950.

Chipping Norton Chamber of Commerce Trades Week 1950. The comic football match.

The RSPCA animal clinic showing animals waiting to be treated. The clinic was situated in Rock Hill. Mrs Grace Packer, wife of Frank Packer, the photographer, ran the clinic for many years, ably assisted by Leonard Morris. All pets were treated at no expense to their owners.

The Girls Friendly Society float at the Chamber of Commerce Trades Week, 1950, including Wendy Burford, Pamela Hawtin, Anne Berry, Eileen Bolter and Pat Carter.

Chipping Norton Football Club 2nd XI 1950/51. From left to right, back row: John Page, Darrel Smith, Dennis Kent, Mr Rose, Peter Grant, Austin Smith, Sid Moulder, John Alder, Ernie Sandles. Seated: Stan Franklin, Bill Aldridge, Ernie Widdows, Jock Hutchison, Claude Edginton.

Chipping Norton Festival of Britain celebrations, 1951. Members of the borough council on the steps of the town hall, Mr Basil Packer with his cine camera on the right.

Festival of Britain celebrations 1951. Mr. W. C. Master's Marauding Mudlarks vs Worth's Worthless Wanderers, a comic football match on the Common.

The fancy dress parade at the Festival of Britain celebrations 1951.

The Marauding Mudlarks in the Festival of Britain parade.

The Children's Fancy Dress Dance at the Norton Hall, December 1951. Norton Hall was being used for events as the town hall had been gutted by fire early in 1950. Teddy Dix and his band played.

The unveiling of the War Memorial and Garden of Remembrance at the bottom of Rock Hill and London Road.

Remembrance Sunday 1951. Present are Lady Mayor Miss Sybil Webb, Town Clerk Mr K. C. E. Holmes, the Mace Bearer, George Hughes and Police Sergeant Charles Kirk, and members of the borough council.

G. R. Hartwell Ltd garage in Horsefair (Note the cottage, now demolished, behind the petrol pumps).

The senior section of the Chipping Norton Keep-Fit Club. From left to right, back row: Janet Withers, Joan Burden, Valerie Bennett, Pat Harding, Joy Newman, Mabel Perry, Ann Slatter, Dorothy Burden, Eileen Bolter. Front row: Jackie Townley, Marian Hoare, Nina Haney, Wendy Burford, Patricia Fletcher.

Children's party given by the British Legion in their clubroom.

St Valentine's Day in Chipping Norton. Miss Flo Hovard, proprietor of the George Inn in New Street tossing hot coins to the children on St Valentine's Day 1953. The children of Chipping Norton used to sing the rhyme 'Please to give me a valentine, I'll be yours if you'll be mine' to the shops and inns of the town before going to school on Valentine's Day. The St Valentine's custom had been observed in Chipping Norton for many generations. Children rose early on that day and by 8 a.m. were ready for school. They formed groups and chanted the St Valentine rhyme outside all the shops and inns until apples, nuts and sweets were thrown to them. This they repeated until they rushed off to school, not daring to be late! This custom was still in use until 1953. Mr Jim Shadbolt, talking to Muriel White, is seen on the left of the picture taking photographs for Mr Frank Packer.

The Girl's Friendly Society choir singing on the town hall steps for May Day 1953. Sheila and Pam Hawtin, Pat Leach, Marian Hoare, Nina Haney are in the front row, along with Girl Guide Anna Watkins, who had presented the mayoress with a bouquet of flowers.

The wartime static water tank being demolished in the town centre in November 1955. A large goldfish abandoned at the Mop fair lived in the tank. Note the shops on the lower market place.

Chipping Norton Grammar School in 1953 before the building of the new hall and kitchen. The bay windows on either side of the main entrance were the school library and the Headmaster's study.

May Day Celebrations. The May Queen, Miss Virginia Thomas, being crowned by the Mayor Col. J. E. S. Chamberlayne on the town hall steps, while members of the GFS entertained the crowd with maypole dancing, ably assisted by the Chipping Norton Silver Band.

The Coronation tea for The Leys held at Craft's Mill in Station Road.

A float decorated by girls from the telephone exchange, waiting in Banbury Road to take part in the parade through the town, including Margaret Hovard, Vera Strong and Mavis Clacy. Mr Cyril Ackerman and his son John are watching the float in the Banbury Road.

New Street children enjoying their tea in the Baptist schoolroom.

Cotswold Crescent celebrations including Coronation Queen Rita Hathaway and her attendants Janice Dilley and Janet Withers.

Coronation Day 1953. Chipping Norton schoolchildren receiving their rulers from the Mayor and Mayoress, Col. J. E. S. Chamberlayne and Mrs Chamberlayne. All Chipping Norton children received either a ruler or a silver teaspoon.

Coronation tea in Over Norton Road.

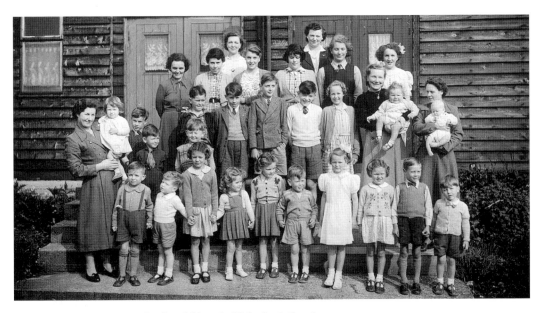

Coronation tea party for the children in Walterbush Road.

The Queen's visit to Chipping Norton.

Crowds waiting on Top Side for the arrival of Queen Elizabeth.

Her Majesty Queen Elizabeth visiting Chipping Norton on her official visit to Oxfordshire on 8 April 1959. She was presented with a length of Bliss tweed.

Senior citizens of the town enjoying a tea in the town hall given by members of the town's fire service to celebrate the Coronation.

Senior citizens enjoying their entertainment in the upper town hall. The ladies of the retained firemen in the town provided the teas.

Verneuil-sur-Avre was twinned with Chipping Norton in the 1950s. This picture shows the farewell dinner for the French visitors' football team from Verneuil-sur-Avre and their supporters in the Co-operative hall.

A visit to the House of Commons by members of the sixth form at Chipping Norton Grammar School. Some of those depicted include Graham Souch, Norman Windsor, Lorna Wheeler, Joy Cripps, Jill Cambray, Mary Allen, Brenda Davies, Hazel Charwood, Rosalind Tidmarsh, Diana Bendle, Douglas Bates, Tony Ambrose, David Miles, Maureen Ball.

Teddy Dix and his band on one of the floats in a parade From left to right, John Beard, Mary Hicks, Valerie Harris and Peter Watkins are with the band, who are Teddy Dix, Les Pickett, Bert Ackerman, Joe Townley and Jack Clapton.

The 1957 Boxing Day meet at the Crown and Cushion Hotel. Mr and Mrs S. D. Wykes, Mayor and Mayoress amongst the Heythrop Hounds. Capt. Ronnie Wallace and Percy Durno with the hounds. The Heythrop Hunt was an offshoot of the Duke of Beaufort's Hunt from 1837 and like the Beaufort, their pinks are green! James Langston, a local landowner, built the kennels in Worcester Road about 1860. Albert Brassey was Master of Fox Hounds from 1873 to 1918 and was succeeded by his son and also his grand-daughter Mrs McKinnon.

The High Street in the 1950s, showing Baxter's butcher's shop, Mrs Brigg's dress shop, the Co-operative chemist's shop, the Co-operative sweet shop and George Smith's electrical shop.

The foyer of the Regent Cinema in New Street, advertising the film *Maytime in Mayfair* with Anna Neagle and Michael Wilding.

Cliff Rogers and Dorothy Randerson in the hall at Chipping Norton Grammar School with members of the youth club.

The 25th Anniversary Dinner at Chipping Norton Grammar School in the school hall May 1953, celebrating twenty-five years of the school. Those depicted include the Headmaster Mr P. W. Martin, Mrs C. King, the Rev. K. St. C. Thomas, Miss Sybil Webb, Ruth and Tom Bunting, Jack Marshall, the Rev. and Mrs Holmes from Churchill, Mr and Mrs Dewar (Headmaster of The Green School, Chipping Norton), Mr and Mrs Stanley Wykes (Headmaster of the Church of England Boy's School in Church Street, Chipping Norton), Gwyneth and George Warrick, Brenda Shadbolt, Aubrey Burden, Pat Wiggins, Peter Robinson, Joyce and Alan Craft, Harry Hovard and Leonard Miles (mathematics teacher at the grammar school).

In 1958/59 Chipperfield's Circus purchased the old sawmill at Heythrop and made it their winter quarters and training ground. The first winter was very cold and the Heythrop farm had little protection from the weather. The eight elephants, at the close of the summer season, were brought to Chipping Norton by train. They were then led up New Street, through the centre of the town and up the Banbury Road to Heythrop. Escorting the elephants were young Dickie Chipperfield and their trainers.

three

The 1960s

Cup winners at the horticultural show. Some of the prize winners include Mr Meredith, Mr Reg Beale from Witney, Mr Leonard Miles, Mrs Maureen Knightall and the winner of the children's cup Elizabeth Craft.

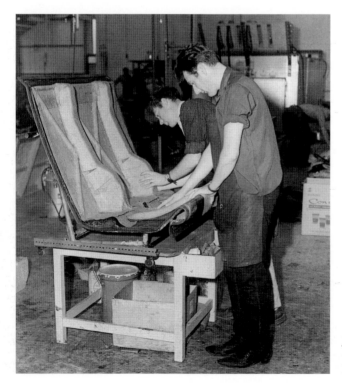

John Grantham and Terry Cox working in the Parker Knoll factory.

Pupils at St Mary's Junior School saying 'goodbye' to their Headmistress Mrs Smith on her retirement from the school, including Barbara Richards, Susan Ryman, Paula Roberts, Rebecca Keene, Adele Balfour, Audrey Brindle, Sarah Hawtin, David Cox, Caroline Harper, Margaret Johnston, Julie Pinfold and Jonathan Hawtin.

Town Mayor Cllr Sholto Major presenting a cup to Margery Sale and Mike Nurden for the winning float from Bliss Mill at the Silver Band Fete.

Michael Morris, Tracey Hicks, Jenny Warmington and friend sitting on the front seats watching the entertainment at the Christmas party of the Tufty Club, 1967.

The Tufty Club Christmas Party 1967 held in the town hall. The Tufty Club was a road safety club for very young children led by Mrs Mary Francis and held regularly in the town hall.

Headmistress Mrs Smith and teacher Tony Aries with their pupils from St Mary's School setting out on a residential holiday.

Sunday school pupils at the Church of England Infant School in Burford Road with their teachers Mr Elliott and Miss Sylvia Rose.

Above: Nativity scene at the Baptist chapel in New Street.

Left: Miss Nellie Jackson cutting her 80th birthday cake in June 1969 with Mrs Mary Francis. Miss Jackson was headmistress of the British School in New Street for many years before her retirement.

Meet of the Heythrop Hounds at Chipping Norton on Boxing Day 1960 outside the Crown & Cushion Hotel. Capt. Ronnie Wallace with the Mayor of Chipping Norton Cllr Sholto Major.

'Uncle Tom Cobberley' on a float at the Silver Band Carnival. The young men all came from Charlbury.

The Wednesday market in Chipping Norton. The road to Market Street from the top of New Street was still open to traffic at that time.

Armistice Parade on the High Street looking towards the town hall steps. Some of those on parade include: George Lamb, Mr Rutter, Mr Norman Bolter, George Hannis, Mr Cleveley, Cyril Allen, Betty Hicks, Stella and Laurie Burden and Mrs George Morris and members of ATC 136 Squadron.

British Legion members' children enjoying a Christmas party in their clubroom.

Swimming Pool Gala. Members of the post office and telephone exchange on their float: Wendy Pratley, Sheila Bartholomew, Dorothy Burden, Nellie Aldridge, Amy Buckingham and Derek Allen as Neptune.

The prize-winning float at the Swimming Pool Carnival in September 1964.

Postman Derek Allen sorting letters at Chipping Norton Post Office.

Songs of Praise recorded at St Mary's church. In the congregation are Heather Leonard and Mrs Latchem.

Tommy Aldridge at work at the rear of his home in College Place.

Round Table members with their float, collecting money for a new minibus. Mayor David Leach is standing on the float. Also pictured are Ron Stares and David Hunt.

Members of the British Legion at Ascot, including Rose Sale, Joan Dix, Stella Burden, Mrs Witts, Gwennie Panting and Joyce Deering.

Women's Institute members enjoying a meal. Some of the members are Mrs Witts, Mrs Elsie Shadbolt, Mrs Deeley, Lorna Brindle, Mrs Maureen Robinson, Mrs Simms, Mrs Ackerman, Mrs Chard, Mrs Daniels, Mrs Phyllis Morse, Mrs Elliott, Mrs Anderson and Miss Ena Neville.

The 2nd Chipping Norton Girl Guides with their Captain Sylvia Rose in the Methodist chapel. Guides include Sarah Hawtin, Pauline Pratley, Sheila Muston, Lynn Sandles, Sharon Hicks, Susan and Julie Eden and Patsy Court.

Chipping Norton School tennis team 1965, sitting outside the school cricket pavilion.

Chipping Norton School hockey team, 1965.

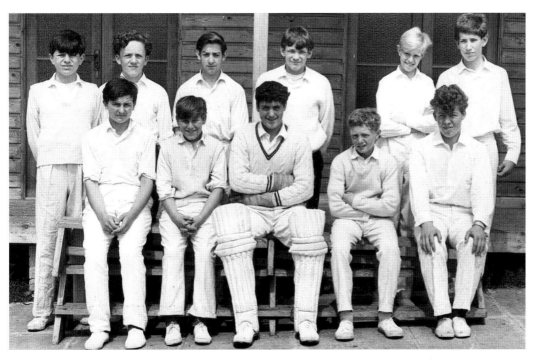

Chipping Norton School U15 cricket team.

Chipping Norton School football team.

Contestants for Miss Chipping Norton at the Norton Hall included Maureen Helmore, Valerie Pickett, Vivienne Spencer and Denise Perry.

Carnival Queen Miss Muriel White with her attendants Diana Balhatchet and Denise Perry.

Sunday school children in fancy dress including Kevin Harding, Alessandro Calden, Sarah Morris, Annalisa Calden, and Miss Sylvia Rose.

Miss Chadwick with the pupils at the Church of England Infant School in Burford Road.

Miss Jenny Allen with gymnasts from Chipping Norton School.

Steam vehicles in the quarry at Chapel House, belonging to Neville Melhuish.

Mr Jim Shadbolt, groundsman, mowing the grass at the Chipping Norton town tennis courts. The outdoor swimming pool was built on this site.

Some of the members of the Chipping Norton Tennis Club: Peter Harding, Pat Wiggins, Wally Haney and Brenda Shadbolt.

Peter Flick instructing members of the 136 Chipping Norton Squadron ATC.

Red Cross members and the Girl Guides on parade on Armistice Sunday going to St Mary's church, led by Mrs Coleman of the Red Cross.

Darts League winners in the town hall, including John and Tony Beard, Michael Dixon, Paul Bennett, Arthur Beasley and Mr Hickman, landlord of the Bunch of Grapes.

The Mayor, Mr P. J. Leach, cutting the first turf for the Parker Knoll factory. Among the onlookers are Bob Brindle, Mrs Leach, John Hannis, Cyril Masters, Charles Withers, Frank Jarvis. Mrs Helen Latcham and Tom Stroud.

Mr Arthur Nockels, Headmaster of Chipping Norton School, receiving a prize at the school fête from the lucky number stall.

National Children's Home Fete with clown Cyril Jackson. The children had presented their Sunny Smile purses.

Chipping Norton Grammar School staff. From left to right, front row: Miss J. Robinson (Headmistress), Miss Jenny Allen, -?-, Miss Betty Harrop, Mrs Ransome, -?-, -?-, -?-, -?-, -?-. Middle row: David Eddershaw, Cliff Rogers, Michael Knightall, -?-, -?-, Mr Taylor, Trevor Easterbrook, Edwin James, Dr E. L.Wright, Mr Benwell. Back row: -?-, Mr Arthur Nockels (Headmaster), Mr Geraint Jones, -?-, Mike Beale, -?-, Mr Ransome, Mr Jefferies, -?-.

Chipping Norton Women's Institute with Mayor Robin Thistlethwayte after presenting a new seat to the people of Chipping Norton.

A traffic jam in New Street outside the old George Inn, with the snack bar on the right-hand side, belonging to Vic Cooper. The Blue Lion public house is still in use.

Cars halted whilst part of Mr Bignall's café wall collapses in the street in June 1969.

Clearing the rubble away after the demolition of the corner shop and Mr Bignell's restaurant.

Webb's department store being demolished. Mrs C. Tomlinson and daughter Karen are waiting to cross the street.

The 'Bomb Site' showing the garden and wall belonging to No. 25 New Street – the home of Mrs Dorothy Shadbolt.

Dr Latcham's house being held up with scaffolding.

FINSBURY PLACE, NEW STREET, Chipping Norton

PETHER & SON

Margaret Bellwood.

A sketch by Margaret Bellwood of Finsbury Place just before demolition.

KINGS HEAD COURT

A sketch of King's Head yard before renovation.

Mayor and Mayoress John and Annie Gripper, 1966. Mr Gripper came to Chipping Norton in 1958 from Guildford where he had been in practice for three years. His veterinary practice was at his home, Glovers House, in Albion Street. Mrs Gripper was the first Brown Owl of the 3rd Chipping Norton Brownie Pack.

Mayor Mr Robin
Thistlethwayte and
Mrs Thistlethwayte.
Mr Thistlethwayte was elected
Mayor in 1964/65 and was the
borough's youngest mayor to
that date, aged twenty-nine. He
was a partner in Alfred Saville &
Sons in Chipping Norton and
resided at the Manor House in
West Street.

A view looking towards the town hall with a Stratford blue bus which called at Chipping Norton
en route to Oxford.

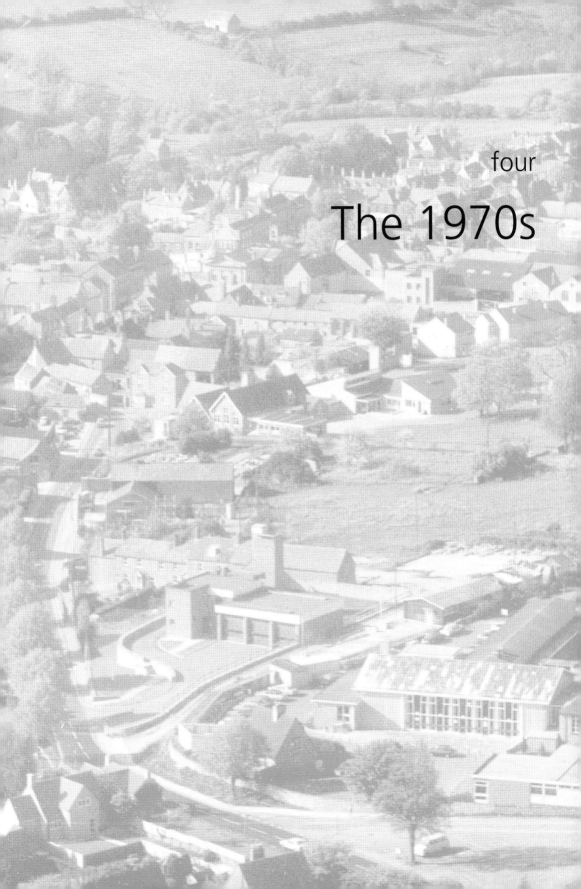

four

The 1970s

Children from Chipping Norton Infants School dressed for the Nativity play, 1970.

Mr Ralph Mann, Head of History at Chipping Norton School, and some fourth-form boys stripping willow bark from a tree on what used to be the Rev. Edward Stone's land, next to the Common brook, near to the Bliss Mill. This could be called the birthplace of the aspirin. Rev. Edward Stone was born in 1702 and lived in Chipping Norton. While living here, he treated a leg wound by wrapping it in willow bark. In doing this he discovered the painkilling and anti-inflammatory properties of the active ingredient of willow bark, salicylic acid. He conducted clinical trials on fifty fever sufferers and presented a paper to the Royal Society in April 1763 called 'An account of the success of the Bark of the Willow in the Cure of Agues.' Many years later, the German drug company Bayer created a stable acetylsalicylic acid, which led to the aspirin.

The last Chipping Norton Borough Council, 1973. From left to right, back row: John Peterkin, John Mitchell, Cyril Masters, John Edginton, Dave Leech, Ronald Stares, Eric Hood, Victor Robinson. Middle row: John Gripper, Mr Cunningham (Town Clerk), John Hannis, Ethel Jackson, Charlie Withers. Front row: Helen Latcham, Paddy Roche, David Eddershaw, John Grantham, David Hunt and John Sale.

The High Street. Premises occupied by J. E. Simms Jewellers & Clockmakers, and the Pearl Assurance Co., before rebuilding as Finefare supermarket in 1970.

The opening of the modernised Co-op grocery store, No. 3 High Street.

The opening of the
Finefare supermarket,
High Street. Store
Manager Mr N. Taylor
hands over a shopping bag
on wheels to the first
customer, Mrs Burnside.

Cup winners at the Horticultural Summer Show 1970 with Mayor Mrs Helen Latcham who presented the prizes. Some of the prize winners were: Mr and Mrs Moyes, Mr Meredith, and the winner of the Children's Cup, Diana Morris.

Post office float at the Swimming Pool Carnival, 1974.

Pupils at Chipping Norton School with their handicrafts at the hobby competitions.

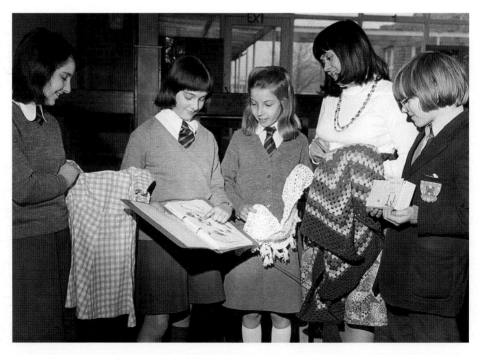

Diana Morris, Susan Knightall, Julie Gardener, Mrs Laura Simper and Steven Heath. Susan is showing Mrs Laura Simper her entry for the hobby competition at Chipping Norton School.

The top of New Street showing Duke's store and the estate agents James Styles & Whitlock. The north side of New Street is still awaiting development.

The Market Square, October, 1977.

A view from Top Side showing New Street and the 'Bomb Site', 1977.

Distons Lane, 1977.

The 1st Chipping Norton Brownie Pack, 1979, with leaders Brenda Morris and Loelia King,
Young Leader Diana Morris and Pack Leader Susan King.

The 2nd Chipping Norton Guide Unit with their leaders Miss Sylvia Rose and Mrs Williams.

Chipping Norton Scout Group with leader John Caswell outside St Mary's church.

Diana Morris receiving her Queen's Guide Award in the Baptist schoolroom from District Commissioner Joan Williams with Molly Wykes, Beryl Jepson and Mayor and Mayoress Mr and Mrs John Grantham.

An aerial view showing Chipping Norton School and the new fire station in May 1976.

A concert given by pupils of Chipping Norton School.

Chipping Norton School first-year netball team, 1977.

Chipping Norton School sixth-form hockey team, 1977.

Members of the St Mary's church choir. From left to right, front row: Peter Ellis, Michael Morris, Philip Allen, Ian Winchester, Jonathan Hawtin, Francis Burroughes (Choirmaster), Rev. T. Wharton, Russell Frost, Ian Carter, Martin Harper, Andrew Ellis and the two Wilson boys. Second row: Karen Herbert, Janine Howling, Alison King, Nicola Carter, Dorothy Willetts, Joan Gomm, Caroline Harper, Andrea Marston, Sarah Hawtin. Back row: Fred Riches, Mr Goodson, Mr Leslie Slade, Mr Frank Barnes, Mr Norman Burbidge, Mr Percy Calcutt and Mr T. Gomm.

An aerial view of St Mary's church showing the Castle Banks and the mount.

Fashion parade given by the Chipping Norton Co-operative Society in the town hall. The commentary is being given by the drapery manager, Mr Edginton.

The finale at the fashion parade was the bridal scene with all the mannequins dressed for a wedding.

Fashion parades were a regular attraction given by the drapery department of the Chipping Norton Co-operative Society. The mannequins were mostly ladies employed in the department. The ladieswear section was hugely popular with clothing being dispatched by the Co-operative vans to the outlying villages. There was also a dressmaking service in the department.

Chipping Norton School from the playing field.

Members of the Chipping Norton School Golf Club.

The Domestic Science room at Chipping Norton School.

The typing class at Chipping Norton School, 1978.

Alderman Charlie Withers and Cllr David Hunt.

Mr Jim Rathbone of Kingham, and his sons Reginald and Fred, with the gates which they made for the Royal Entrance to the Ascot racecourse.

Opposite above: Post early for Christmas! The children of Chipping Norton Infants School.

Opposite below: Chipping Norton Darts League final and presentation in the town hall.

Members of the Chipping Norton Trefoil Guild with the seat in St Mary's churchyard which was given in memory of Mrs Mollie Wykes. Mollie is remembered with great affection for the many years she gave to Guiding in Chipping Norton. Some of the Trefoil members depicted are: Nora McDowell, Brenda Morris, Sylvia Bunce, Sylvia Rose, Joan Williams, Delma Paish, Flo Souch, Enid Eden, Sheila Parker, Mary Jones, Leah Fowler, Joy Newman, Shirley Floyd, Betty Gardener, Mrs Atkins, Angela Dukes and Mrs Muston.

The 1st Chipping Norton Brownies and their leaders Madeleine Rickard and Brenda Morris in 1994.